Illusions

Illusions

Poetry & Art for the Young at Heart

by Charles Ghigna
Illustrated by Chip Ghigna

"We are such stuff as dreams are made on..."
—William Shakespeare

for Charlotte and Christopher

RESOURCE *Publications* • Eugene, Oregon

ILLUSIONS
Poetry & Art for the Young at Heart

Wipf & Stock
An Imprint of Wipf and Stock Publishers
199 W. 8th Ave., Suite 3
Eugene, OR 97401

www.wipfandstock.com

PAPERBACK ISBN: 978-1-7252-6013-9
HARDCOVER ISBN: 978-1-7252-6007-8
EBOOK ISBN: 978-1-7252-6008-5

Manufactured in the U.S.A.

Cover art by Chip Ghigna

~ *Contents* ~

Life's An Illusion

Life's an illusion.
A dream on the wing.
A summerful fancy.
A winter of spring.

Life is a circus.
A high-wire act.
A tiptoe of balance.
A never-look-back.

Life is a garden.
A path in the wood.
An apple tree tease
From shouldn't to should.

Life is a lover.
A promise to keep.
A wish for tomorrow
In a daydream of sleep.

Daydreamer

I'm going on vacation in my mind.
I'm going there to see what I might find.
If I'm not back by half past eight,
Please don't stay. Please don't wait.

Please don't call. Please don't write.
I'm going going out of sight.
Please don't cry and carry on.
I'm going going going -- gone.

Inspiration

It is every
thing
you think it is.

It is the end
of the tunnel
and the light up ahead.

It is the sound
of the wind
and the silence of the night.

It is the sun
and the moon
and the memory.

It is the eye
and the hand
and the mouth.

It is the present
the future
and the past.

It is here.
It is there.
It is gone.

Art

Art is undefinable,
A mystery of creation
Inspired by a pigment
Of your imagination.

One

Open the door
A little more.
Feast your eyes
On the skies.

The wonder.
The glory.
The sweet
Endless story

Of all
That is
Sacred
And wise.

Within us.
Without us.
Above us.
Below.

The journey.
The ebb.
The answer.
The flow.

The earth.
The sea.
The stars
And the sky

Tell us
the tale
Of the sparrow
And whale

Of the who
And the where
And the
Why.

Nothing
Begins.
Nothing
Is done.

The present
The past
And the future
Are one.

Earth Bound

In the vastness of time and space
We ride this one little star
Never stopping to ponder our fate
Or how fragile and fleeting we are.

Treescape

Stare into the face of Nature
Till the forest owns your eyes.
Search beneath the surface shine
Until her depth dispels your lies.

Climb your stare upon her trees
Until you see all shades of green.
Cast your vision past itself
Until your sight becomes the scene.

Moon Tree

Moon tree
stares up
at the night

makes her
wish upon
a star

holds darkness
in her leaves
like a secret

waits for morning
to come share her
gift of light.

Suddenly September

A crisp cool
sky blue
lazy day
in the middle
of summer
and suddenly
the leaves
shimmer
with a golden secret
and the breeze
whispers low
"It's autumn."

Indigo

They are the children
who sit by the window,
their minds and their hearts
full of love.

They are the children
who sit by the window,
their thoughts
in the clouds high above.

In dreams drawn by pixies,
they stream from the sixties
to lead a new band
through the crowd.

They dance and they hum,
they beat their own drum
in songs
so silently loud.

They paint and they play
the night into day.
They color the sky
orange blue.

Through sunshine
and thunder,
they sit and they wonder
of new worlds yet to come true.

Aries Sideshow

Like a magnet
under the magician's table,
the swan's reflection
pulls her across the lake,

while deep inside the brush
an unseen hand
pulls rabbits
out of rabbits.

Tell Me

about how you lost
your interest
in words,

about how you feel
so full
of them

you think you might
break out
in red letters,

think if you hear
another word
you will scream,

will run blindly
into the woods
and hide,

will dip your finger
into the stream
and write your final line,

will lie on your back
and stare up
at the stars,

will run home
through the dark
and sit alone by the fire

until someone who cares
comes to your side
and says, "tell me."

The House on the Cliff by the Sea

I come Ishmael to you from the midnight sea.
The gray fog clings, a pasted beard, to my cheeks.
It grows wild from my chin around the world.

You raise the lantern
higher to your face
and stare into the dark at a dream.

The window holds you
like a portrait hung against the sky.
I come bringing morning in my beard.

Optical Allusion

Like the baby who first
sees himself in the mirror
and thinks he has met a stranger,

we shuffle through the old photographs
searching for the one we used to be.
But no matter how many times we smiled,

no matter how many times
we combed our hair and acted coy,
no matter how many times

the camera made us small,
we can only guess the fate
of this smiling, young stranger

who once resembled us,
this smiling, young stranger
we hold like a fortune in our hands.

Hands That See

Your hands see
your eyes feel
fantasies
beyond the real

clouds of blue
skies of white
painting color
into light

dreams awake
the sleeping mind
break the bonds
that keep us blind

you see life
in grains of sand
you hold light
within your hand

It Would Be Easy

to write of love
if I could build
a mirror
in every poem
and hand
each one
to you.

Present Light

If I could
hold light
in my hand

I would
give it
to you

and watch it
become
your shadow.

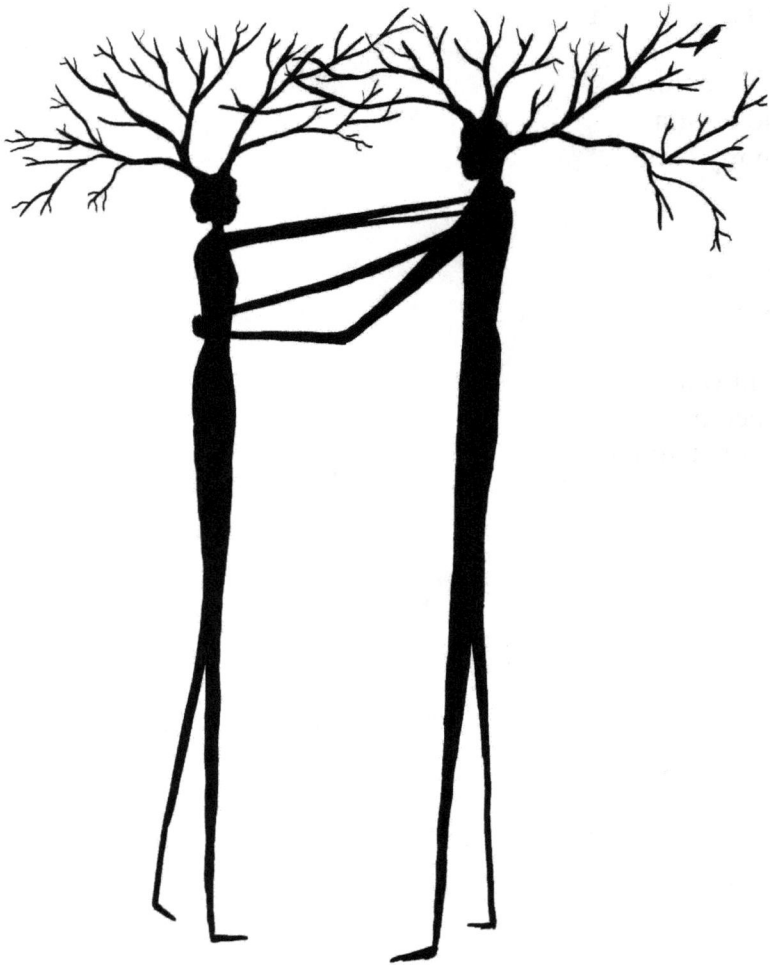

Royal Love

You treat Love
like a king.

You crown him
with your smile.

You rule him
with your kiss.

You make him wish
you were his queen.

You make Love
jealous.

Your Song

sings always in me
even when you are silent,
even when you are away.

To me there is no sound
as soft as you,
no voice on earth

that gives my feet such wings,
no whispered prayer
filled with so much promise.

Your voice is the pillow
on which I rest my heart,
the blanket with which

I warm my dreams,
the bed in which my soul
learns its nightly lesson
of everlasting love.

Ars Longa, Vita Brevis

Like the sculptor
who chips away
at what is not
the sculpture,
your life
is in your hands,
the pure
imperfect stone
waiting for its
daily touch,
the gentle tap,
the savored strike
toward mass
and space
that form
the perfect past,
your tribute
to the art
of living.

Be Still

Be still in the world wherever you are,
listen to life's lullaby;
the heartbeat, the breathing, the giving, receiving,
the sun and the moon and the star.

They all shine true through the essence of you,
a beacon of boundless light;
the father, the mother, the sister, the brother,
all are within you tonight.

Let the flow of the seas, the lilt of the breeze,
the rush and the calm of all time
carry your dreams along rivers and streams
and let you be still where you are.

Charles Ghigna lives in a treehouse in the middle of Alabama. He is the author of more than 100 books from **Disney, Random House, Scholastic, Simon & Schuster, Time Inc.** and other publishers. He has written more than 5,000 poems for children and adults. His work appears in anthologies, newspapers, and magazines ranging from *The New Yorker* and *Harper's* to *Highlights* and *Cricket*. He served as poet-in-residence at the Alabama School of Fine Arts, instructor of creative writing at Samford University, and as a nationally syndicated feature writer for Tribune Media. More information at **CharlesGhigna.com**

Chip Ghigna lives in Homewood, Alabama. His paintings appear in galleries, corporations, and private collections throughout the U.S. and France. See more of his art at **ChipGhigna.com**

*   *   *

Final Lines

Artist. Poet.
Creative minds.
We spend our lives
Making lines.

We paint.
We write.
All day.
All night.

Lines connect.
Father. Son.
Lines that bind
To make us one.

www.ingramcontent.com/pod-product-compliance
Lightning Source LLC
Chambersburg PA
CBHW051049030426

42339CB00006B/263